WRITTEN BY
JEFF LUCAS

Every

God's Playlist

Published 2021 by Waverley Abbey Resources. Waverley Abbey Resources
is the operating name of CWR, Waverley Abbey House, Waverley Lane,
Farnham, Surrey GU9 8EP, UK
Registered Charity No. 294387 Registered Limited Company No. 1990308

Concept development, editing, design and production by Waverley Abbey
Resources.
Front cover image: Adobe Stock
Printed in the UK by Bishops Printers

MIX
Paper from
responsible sources
FSC® C015900

WAVERLEY ABBEY
RESOURCES

OPERATING NAME OF **CWR**

How to get the best out of *Life Every Day*

- Ideally, carve out a regular time and place each day, with as few distractions as possible. Ask God what He has to say to you.

- Read the Bible passages suggested in the 'Read' references. (As tempting as it is, try not to skip the Bible reading and get straight into the notes.)

- The 'FOCUS:' reference then gives you one or two verses to look at in more detail. Consider what the reading is saying to you and what challenges that may bring.

- Each day's comments are part of an overall theme. Try to recall what you read the previous day so that you maintain a sense of continuity.

- Spend time thinking about how to apply what God has said to you. Ask Him to help you do this.

- Pray the prayer at the end as if it were your own. Perhaps add your own prayer in response to what you have read and been thinking about.

Join in the conversation on Facebook
facebook.com/jefflucasuk

he God who knows

Read:
Psalm 3:1–2
2 Samuel 15:1–14

FOCUS

'LORD, how many are my foes! How many rise up against me!'
(Psa. 3:1)

t's the last straw that breaks the camel's back, so the saying goes. Sometimes the challenges of life tack up together and leave us feeling overwhelmed, anicked and fearful. Certainly, that was David's xperience when he wrote this psalm. He was a ugitive from his own son, Absalom, who had gathered n army of supporters and was set on seizing the rone and killing his father. Their relationship had een troubled for some time, and David had not andled his family problems well, but he was still njoying great success when, suddenly, Absalom ommitted this ultimate act of betrayal.

This was not unusual in ancient times. Sennacherib, he king of Assyria who laid siege to Jerusalem, was illed by two of his own sons (2 Chron. 32:21). As a ather, I cannot begin to imagine the devastating pain avid felt, realising his own child had done everything e could to usurp him and wanted him dead. And then, alking up the Mount of Olives, there was further gony, as one of Saul's relatives, Shimei, cursed David nd pelted him with insults and stones.

Faith can seem futile when life batters us, but e love and serve Jesus, who knows well what that eels like. Bowed below the gargantuan pressure of ethsemane, with the physical and spiritual agonies of ne cross ahead, He confessed He was overwhelmed rith sorrow (Mark 14:34). When we feel the same ay, we come to a God who has more than felt these ressures, and who understands.

rayer: When life brings multiple challenges, I come to ou. You know what life can feel like, Lord Jesus, Amen.

Faith can
seem futile

God our shield, who lifts our head

....

FOCUS

'But you, LORD, are a shield around me, my glory, the One who lifts my head high.' (Psa. 3:3)

Yesterday, we saw a picture of David in a place of shame and despair. Here, he celebrates the God who protected him – as he speaks of God as his shield he echoes the promise of God to Abraham. David also used the picture of God as shield when he was rescued from Saul's murderous campaign (2 Sam. 22:3). He also uses a most beautiful, tender phrase, grateful that God had lifted his head high. Commentators believe David was contrasting the dark day when his head was down and he was an object of mockery, with the loving and strengthening encouragement he had received from the Lord.

When the Bible speaks of lifting our heads, we see a picture of moving from despair to hope. 'When these things begin to take place, stand up and lift up your heads, because your redemption is drawing near', Jesus taught (Luke 21:28).

When I read these verses, I think of a loving parent tenderly comforting a sobbing child, placing a hand beneath their chin, gently lifting their head to look into their eyes. Surely this is what our God is like, as He gives 'endurance and encouragement' (Rom. 15:5).

When we feel vulnerable, or we've failed badly and we feel deeply ashamed, our heads go down. If that's where you are today, may you know God does not stand aside, aloof and indifferent. Because He is your shield, your life is still in His hands. When you are downcast, He wants to lift your head and for you to know hope again.

this is what
our God
is like

Prayer: My God, my protector, You surround me. When I am fearful or ashamed, lift my head, so I might see You in that moment by faith. Amen.

God our sustainer and sleep

Read:
Psalm 3:5–8
Proverbs 3:24

FOCUS

'I lie down and sleep;
I wake again,
because the LORD
sustains me.'
(Psa. 3:5)

Night prayer, known in the liturgy as Compline (from the Latin *completorium*, the completion of the working day) has been practised throughout Christian history. As David affirms that God 'sustains' him, there is a strong connection between that truth and his ability to sleep, even though, as we've seen, he was in a season of battling troubles on every side.

The shadows of the night accelerate our capacity for fear. Surely all of us have experienced the disorientating lack of perspective that the small hours bring. We toss and turn fitfully, our minds churning as we ponder terrible possibilities. Sometimes, when the sun rises, clarity is restored, and we wonder why we were so fearful and restless. As David talks about God the sustainer, he uses words that speak of present and future hope: literally, 'the Lord will sustain me'. Perhaps the essence of this idea is captured in the child's prayer, 'Now I lay me down to sleep, I pray the Lord my soul to keep.' The original version of that prayer was written by Thomas Addison, the co-founder of the Spectator. It was published in the magazine in 1711: 'When I lay me down to sleep, I recommend myself to His care; when I wake, I give myself up to His direction.'

So, why not try night prayer? As a suggestion for what we might use at the end of the day, our prayer today is adapted from the *New Zealand Prayer Book*. Live well today, and rest well tonight, safe in the sustaining God.

Prayer: Lord, it is night after a long day. What has been done has been done; what has not been done has not been done; let it be. Amen.

'I recommend myself to His care'

Read:
Psalm 4:1–8
1 John 5:13–14

Weekend

The God who hears me

All this talk of night prayer and sleep leads us forward to Psalm 4, where again David affirms he is going to get a good night's rest: 'In peace I will lie down and sleep, for you alone, Lord, make me dwell in safety.' And he reveals another reason for his peaceful slumber; God hears him, a truth David declared earlier in Psalm 3:4.

It can be difficult to find (or be) a friend with a truly listening ear. We all live very conscious of our own strengths and weaknesses, challenges and blessings, and can be tempted to engage in one-sided conversations, talking endlessly about ourselves. Then pausing for breath, we only half listen to what the other person is saying, because we're busily framing our next thought about us! But the God we serve listens, and then, according to John in his epistle, He responds – the word John uses means 'to give heed'. When we talk to God, He is engaged and responsive. Surely reminding ourselves of that truth should nudge us to talk to Him more?

To ponder: What difference does the truth that God listens and hears make to us?

the God we serve listens

WAVERLEY ABBEY
COLLEGE

Higher Education Programmes 2021-22

Spiritual Formation Faculty

MA Spiritual Formation

PG Dip Spiritual Formation

PG Cert

- Chaplaincy
- Mentoring and Coaching
- Pastoral Care
- Spiritual Direction

BA (Hons) Top-up

EMCC
European Mentoring &
Coaching Council

QAA Reviewed
Quality Assurance Agency
for Higher Education

Counselling Faculty

MA Therapeutic Counselling and
Psychotherapy

MA Counselling

BA (Hons) Counselling

Dip HE in Counselling

Leadership Faculty

MA in Public Leadership (distance
learning programme)

This programme is subject to validation
Launching in January 2022

We also offer Continuing Professional Development short courses in Spiritual
Formation and Counselling, including Counselling Supervision training.

To find out more call **01252 784731**

or visit **waverleyabbeycollege.ac.uk**

or email **admissions@waverleyabbeycollege.ac.uk**

Always heard

We call it a dead spot, and we have a couple of them in our home. It's that area where the signal for a mobile phone drops, and so suddenly the conversation is interrupted. 'Can you hear me? Hello? Are you there?' we call, while walking around at speed in the hope that connection will be restored. Our relationship with God can feel like that, especially when we've been hoping an oft-repeated prayer would be answered, but there's little sign of a breakthrough. The psalmist David had many troubles in his life – Psalm 18 was probably written towards the end of his life. He was celebrating God's deliverance from his enemies, including his jealous predecessor, Saul. As David gives thanks, he affirms once again that God has consistently heard him.

Jesus celebrated the intimacy of His relationship with the Father when faced with the challenge of a dead Lazarus and his two grieving sisters. The raising had obviously been a matter of prayer before Jesus ever arrived in Bethany and, once there, He gives thanks for the knowledge the Father has heard Him, and always heard him. Filled with that assurance, Jesus commanded Lazarus to come out, and the eye-popping miracle followed.

We don't always get the response we want when we come to God. In Bethany, death was sent packing. In Gethsemane, Jesus asked for the cup of suffering to be removed, yet to no avail. But our confidence as we walk through life is found in this truth: we are always heard.

Prayer: Father, You listen to me, my words, my heart. I am grateful. Amen.

Read:
Psalm 18:1–6
John 11:42

FOCUS
'From his temple he heard my voice; my cry came before him, into his ears.'
(Psa. 18:6)

We don't always get the response we want

Hearing our tears

FOCUS

'Away from me, all you who do evil, for the LORD has heard my weeping.'
(Psa. 6:8).

Yesterday, we celebrated the truth that God hears us when we call. As we turn to Psalm 6, however, we discover more about God's capacity to listen – He 'hears' our tears. In this psalm, which is generally thought to be a lament of David as he wrestled with ongoing illness, there is utter desperation and complaints of horrible agony. Yet in the midst of it all, David affirms his belief that his cries reach God's ears.

Surely there are times when we just don't have words to frame coherent prayers. Suffering can render us speechless – one reason for my increasing appreciation for well-framed liturgy. But prayer is more than words. Tears shed, murmurs of pain, and even just silence can all be offerings of prayer, because they come from the heart.

There are times when we come to God with little to say, but are determined to be with Him anyway. We can't find words to express how we feel, either because they seem inadequate, or we're just too weary to put a sentence together. When that happens, we should come regardless, and offer Him our silence. The aching heart, the shed tear, or the simple one word cry from our hearts, 'Help!', all these are heard by our attentive God, who lists our tears on a scroll (Psa. 56:8). And sometimes our prayers are 'wordless groans' (Rom. 8:26). Don't let your lack of words prevent you from intentionally being in the presence of God; for the One who can hear our voices also tunes in to our hearts.

his cries reach God's ears

Prayer: When there is nothing useful to say, help me just to want to be with You, faithful God. Amen.

God our refuge

Read:
Psalm 7:1–17
1 Samuel 22:6–15

FOCUS

'LORD my God, I take refuge in you; save and deliver me from all who pursue me.'
(Psa. 7:1)

When a prisoner escapes, or a wanted criminal is on the run, every resource available is used to track the fugitive down. Sniffer dogs, helicopters and bands of law enforcement officers coordinate their efforts to bring the suspect to heel.

As a young man, David was the object of a massive manhunt. Enraged and deranged because David had become a national hero, King Saul was relentless in his pursuit of him, violently attacking him personally and engaging his troops in a mission driven by jealousy and insecurity. It was Ahimelech, the high priest at Nob, who defended David to Saul, and questioned why he was accusing such a loyal and honest man. That conversation cost Ahimelech and the priests who served with him their lives. Saul's furious pursuit and accusatory stance towards David continued. It's thought David was referring to this season in this psalm, although we're not certain, because we don't actually know what a *shiggaion* (a word used in the introduction) is, and also there's no biblical character whom we can identify as 'Cush the Benjamite'. Most commentators believe this refers to Saul because he was a son of Kish.

Falsely accused and fleeing for his life, David appeals to God as his judge. He also celebrates God once again as his shield and refuge. He knows he is not alone, not even in his hour of greatest need: God has been reliably there before, and He will be reliably there again. And as for David, so for us.

God has been reliably there before

Prayer: Lord, I praise You because You are my shield, my refuge, who hears my cry. Amen.

Satan accuses, God is our refuge

David was battling against false accusations – and so do we, as followers of Jesus. I'm not one of those Christians who sees the devil behind every problem, but the Bible speaks to us repeatedly about an enemy who wants to undermine God's grace – and he does that with accusation. Satan uses accusation so much, he is even named in its honour, because the word Satan means 'accuser'. Old Testament writers occasionally refer to their human enemies as 'satans'. The psalmists refer five times to the human 'satans' opposing them (Psa. 38:20; 71:13; 109:4,20,29). Satan is also history's most prolific prosecutor. He has handled cases against Job, Joshua and David. In the wilderness, he came against the Lord Jesus. Through the Pharisees, he accused and blasphemed the Holy Spirit. If the satanic attorney will point the finger at everyone – even the great judge Himself – don't you think that he'll try to pull the same stunt on us?

Considering we are the people who believe in the finished work of Christ at the cross, and the wonderful availability of full and free forgiveness through His shed blood, too many Christians live like shame addicts. Perhaps you're one of them, and your head and heart are downcast because you don't 'feel' forgiven. Accusation torments you. Accepting forgiveness from God is not, however, contingent on what we feel, but rather on the fact of Jesus' finished work, which we accept by faith. As we'll see, when we feel accused, He is our refuge.

Prayer: I stand not in the dock of accusation but on the promises of Your forgiveness, and all because of grace, loving God. Amen.

Read:
Revelations 12:1–12
1 Peter 5:8–11

FOCUS

'For the accuser of our brothers and sisters, who accuses them before our God day and night, has been hurled down.' (Rev. 12:10)

the finished
work of Christ
at the cross

Our refuge: it's personal

Read:
Psalm 7:1
Psalm 11:1–7

FOCUS

'LORD my God, I take refuge in you; save and deliver me from all who pursue me.'
(Psa. 7:1)

Browsing the shelves of a bookshop, I realised there is no shortage of so-called self-help books, proffering advice on how to live our lives: how we can get out of debt, banish worry, be more confident or enjoy greater success. And then I turn to the Bible, and discover a God who offers peace and safety when accusation comes. But there's no call just to pursue security and calm in and of themselves, separate from a relationship with God. Jesus offers us peace, but makes it quite clear this peace is *in* Him, discovered in connection with Him, as He teaches us His rhythm. Peace is not an abstract emotion: it's the result of personal interaction with God. The same is true when we think of God being our refuge – the psalmist says that he takes refuge *in* God. When we feel condemned we find a place of safety not only in the promises of God, but *in* His presence. We run to Him like scared children, seeking protection and comfort.

We're reminded that Christianity is far more than a vague belief system or a commitment to follow a set of moral principles. To use language so familiar it can lack impact, the Christian life is a relationship, a daily faith walk with the risen, living Christ. Theories about Him don't provide a refuge for us. He does. That doesn't suggest we will experience an epic encounter every time we approach Him; but it does promise that as we draw near, He draws near to us. Because He is close, we are ultimately safe and secure.

the Christian life is a relationship

Prayer: Father God, help me to seek You, rather than just the blessing that You offer.

Read:
**Deuteronomy
33:1–27**
Psalm 144:1–2

Our refuge and the everlasting arms

Recently, we have lived with a greater awareness of death. During the height of the Covid crisis in 2020, staggering daily death tolls were announced. Generally we try to avoid the subject, but many Christians in other parts of the world live much closer to mortality, as they battle against disease, persecution and poverty on a daily basis. And believers in previous generations were more aware of pain and suffering as well. As we see a dual picture of God as refuge and hear that 'underneath are the everlasting arms', we're reminded of His awesome power. When the metaphor of God's arms appears in Scripture, it refers to God's mighty strength. Charles Spurgeon, the great Baptist preacher, taught this verse speaks of the Lord not only tenderly carrying us, but being there however low we fall, because His arms are 'underneath'. His power and attentive care are everlasting, forever. In Christ, we are not only cradled in God's care now, but for always.

To ponder: What would you say to a believer who is terrified of dying?

Weekend

His awesome power

Our refuge: liturgy

Read:
Psalm 91:1–2
Acts 4:23–31

FOCUS

'I will say of the LORD, "He is my refuge and my fortress, my God, in whom I trust."'
(Psa. 91:2)

I don't come from a church tradition that uses liturgy very much. I'm sad to confess that in my early years of ministry, when zeal sometimes morphed into thoughtless arrogance, I dismissed liturgy as wooden and hollow, which was a thoughtless generalisation. While I'm still not a fan of the sonorous voice that some Christian leaders adopt when leading a liturgical act of worship, I believe liturgy can be a source of strength and blessing. We saw earlier that sometimes life renders us speechless and, exhausted by the struggle, we can't find words to frame a prayer. Sometimes I don't pray because I just can't think of what to say. The theologically rich, carefully crafted words created by someone else, perhaps hundreds of years ago or more, can strengthen our prayers during those seasons.

As the psalmist says, 'I will say of the Lord', and then, 'My God' he is making a declaration about God being his refuge – his affirmation makes his belief about God personal to him. Surely faith is strengthened when we stand shoulder to shoulder with other believers, joining our voices in unified prayer and speaking out the words of the creeds. Those of us who enjoy more informal contemporary worship styles would be nourished by creative, biblical liturgy. And regardless of what form of worship is used in your church, why not speak out the declaration of the psalmist during your devotions today? As you verbalise truth, may your heart be warmed and encouraged.

liturgy can be a source of strength and blessing

Prayer: God, you are my God. This day, this moment, I love You and will serve You all my days. Amen.

A very present help

When Steven Spielberg produced promotional materials for the classic movie *ET* (surely the kindliest looking alien) it stated that the hapless little green chap was stranded on earth, 3 million light years from home – 17 quintillion miles, quite a trek. Had ET have phoned home, his long distance bill would have been very significant!

Some people, including Christians, view God like that – He is watching us, but from a distance, as the song made famous by Bette Midler says. But the psalmist celebrates that God is near, an 'ever-present help in trouble'. I've written about this before, but it's so important we understand that, while God is 'out there', He is also right here too. In the Lord's prayer, we say He is our Father, who is in heaven, but a better translation would be 'in the heavens' – and 'the heavens' include the air immediately around our bodies. Without this knowledge, prayer becomes worse than a long distance call: we can feel a very long way away from Him.

In what some commentators call a psalm of confidence, the writer here is saying his confidence does not come from an expectation of an easy life. Rather, come what may, it stems from the fact he will never be abandoned or alone. Throughout the pages of Scripture, God so frequently assures His nervous people that He is with them. Perhaps you find yourself in a place of uncertainty and fear – trouble is around or ahead. May this truth strengthen you: God is close to you.

Prayer: Lord, you are close, beside me, before me, behind me, ever-present. May that truth shape the way I think and live. Amen.

Read:
Psalm 46:1–2
Psalm 145:1–21

FOCUS

'God is our refuge and strength, an ever-present help in trouble.' (Psa. 46:1)

God is near

Our refuge, whatever comes our way

FOCUS

'Therefore we will not fear, though the earth give way and the mountains fall into the heart of the sea.' (Psa. 46:2)

It was a terrifying phone call. Our daughter Kelly was in Indonesia, working alongside her husband Ben in Banda Acheh, the city devastated by the Boxing Day tsunami in 2004 – 170,000 people were killed along that coastline. Kelly called to tell us there had been a major earthquake and many had been injured – they were heading to the hospital to help out as volunteers. Later, they shared the utter terror they had felt as the ground shook and the hotel they had been staying in threatened to collapse.

When the psalmist talks about trouble and fear, he uses extreme examples of cataclysmic threat – the earth giving way, the mountains falling into the heart of the sea – he is pondering apocalyptic tragedies that he is pondering. Elsewhere in the book of Psalms, we see extreme worst cases scenarios used. In Psalm 3, which we considered earlier, David says, 'I will not fear though tens of thousands assail me on every side (Psa. 3:6). Because God is his refuge, he is confident and refuses to let terror paralyse him.

Some of us go through life with a sense of dread. We develop some minor symptoms, and nervously scan the internet to see what terrible disease is blighting us (not a good thing to do, and I can speak from experience). Someone once said they had spent their whole lives afraid of countless possibilities, most of which never happened. But if calamity does come, and we are not assured it never will, this truth is firm: God will be with us as our refuge.

God is his refuge

Prayer: Help me to remember Your promises, when all is shaking and uncertain, Your Word is true. Amen.

Refuge and sanctuary

Claiming 'sanctuary' was an ancient custom in medieval Britain. A fleeing criminal could run to the nearest church, and claim protection and safety for up to forty days. This six-week period allowed for negotiation or, perhaps, if the fugitive had fallen out of favour with the king, reconciliation. Hauling someone out of sanctuary was a crime, punishable by death. Imagine the relief to hear the thick oak door of a church close behind you, and know that you were safe, you'd found sanctuary. The sanctuary principle is based on five passages in the Bible that describe 'cities of refuge', (Numbers 35:6–28; Deuteronomy 4:41–43, 19:1–13; and Joshua 20). They were ordained by God, as places where people could be safe while tempers cooled and facts were gathered.

We saw yesterday that God is closer than close, but just as a fugitive would need to make the effort to flee to one of the 'safe' cities, so surely we need to be intentional about drawing near to God. Fear can be an obstacle to spiritual initiatives. When troubles come, we're tempted to dash into fear, sprint into panic, and charge into reactions that often cause great damage to ourselves and others. Running to God in prayer can be our last resort, rather than our first.

I'd love to learn how to 'take refuge' in God, rather than meandering in worry; when I fail, I'd like to run to Him rather than sink in the quicksand of shame. When we are afraid, let's run to Him, not from Him.

Prayer: When I am afraid, I will come to You, loving God. Amen.

Read:
Psalm 142:1–5
Jeremiah 17:1–18

FOCUS

'I cry to you, Lord; I say, "You are my refuge, my portion in the land of the living.' (Psa. 142:5)

God is closer than close

Choosing the refuge of His wings

Read:
Psalm 91:1–4
Matthew 23:37–39

FOCUS

'He will cover you with his feathers, and under his wings you will find refuge.'
(Psa. 91:4)

I know, we're spending quite a lot of time considering God as our refuge, and that's because it is such a frequently used image in the book of Psalms, occurring forty times in the ESV translation. When we make God our refuge, we scurry to Him like chicks running to their mother hen, nestling under her wings. In a very beautiful metaphor (the picture is obviously not meant to be taken literally, since God is not a bird!) and one used a number of times in the Old Testament (cf. Exod. 19:4; Deut. 32:10–11; Psa. 5:11–12; Psa. 17:8; Psa. 63:8) we have a picture of warmth and security in God. But when Jesus used similar imagery, His heart was heavy, because He was speaking about the city of Jerusalem. The prophet Isaiah had spoken about God's desire to shelter Jerusalem: 'Like birds hovering overhead, the LORD Almighty will shield Jerusalem; he will shield it and deliver it' (Isa. 31:5). He had been long-suffering and patient with the inhabitants of that city. Jesus says *'How often* I have longed to gather your children together' (Matt. 23:37, my italics). But despite repeated appeals, they had resisted God's call.

We've already seen that underneath are the everlasting arms, and above are His 'wings' – but in receiving that promise, let's be quick to respond to call when He speaks. Today, let's have open hearts, eager to hear, swift to do what God says without delay. Just as Jesus 'longed' for Jerusalem, so He longs for us.

we have a picture of warmth and security in God

Prayer: I'm grateful for Your heart that longs for me, seeks to gather me, Lord. When Your call is hard, help me to remember that longing. Amen.

Read:
Psalm 91:1–10
Psalm 124:1–8

Rescuer from set traps

Minding my own business during a midweek Bible study and prayer meeting, I was suddenly jolted by an announcement from the platform. An elderly lady was calling my name, requesting that I come forward to allow the church to pray for me. 'Young man', she said (this was a long time ago), 'I feel that God wants me to warn you that in the next few days, a temptation is coming your way and, if you succumb to it, you will ruin your marriage, your ministry – everything you hold dear. Be warned, and be ready.' Sure enough, when I travelled to another area to preach in a local church conference, that temptation presented itself. The details aren't important, but forewarned meant I was forearmed and enabled to make the right choice. I had been saved from a trap. Some Christians have an inflated view of the devil, but we should know the enemy is an agent of temptation as well as the accuser. But as we walk closely with God, He can and will deliver us, 'from the fowler's snare'.

To ponder: If a trap was to be set for you, what might it be?

He can and will deliver us

Angelic commander

FOCUS

'For he will command his angels concerning you to guard you in all your ways.' (Psa. 91:11)

We Christians are eager to find confirmation of our faith, especially when it comes to God's supernatural intervention. At times that has meant we've eagerly swallowed news of a miraculous healing that turned out to be anything but. And we've all heard those stories of angelic appearances, where a hapless Christian motorist, stranded on the hard shoulder of a motorway, is assisted by a smiling, slightly fluorescent passerby who repairs their broken fan belt and then suddenly disappears. Sadly, these stories can lead us into cynicism, especially when the suspected angel turns out to be a friendly local farmer.

But let's be clear: angels do exist: emissaries under God's command, involved in the protection of His people. Whether we all have 'guardian' angels personally assigned to us is unclear and unproven from Scripture. In Daniel's story, an angel protects him in the lions' den (Dan. 6:22); another protects Shadrach, Meshach, and Abednego in the fiery furnace (Dan. 3:28). What we do know is that God's care for His children is demonstrated as the angels celebrate salvation (Luke 15:10), carry those who die in Christ to heaven (Luke 16:22), and are eager to watch the progress of the gospel (1 Pet. 1:12). The Bible doesn't, however, encourage us to seek out angels, or to attempt to commune with them. But in making a point about hospitality, the writer to the Hebrews reminds us that angels do interact and involve themselves in our lives. Thank God!

God's care for His children is demonstrated

Prayer: Lord God, as I remember that there are armies of angels doing good, help me to remember I live on a battlefield planet. Amen.

Angelic commander – but a truth misused

Read:
Psalm 91:11–16
Luke 4:1–12

FOCUS

*'They will lift you up
in their hands, so
that you will not
strike your foot
against a stone.'*
(Psa. 91:12)

Yesterday we celebrated the truth that God is the commander of angels. But truth can so easily be distorted. Christians routinely misquote Scripture, take it out of context, or misuse it to justify their actions. The abusive Christian spouse apologises for their bruising behaviour and then insists their victim has to forgive them and continue in the relationship, regardless of the continual hurt that has emerged. The bullying leader accuses his critics of being divisive and demands they maintain unity, using Scripture as a shield to stop anyone questioning him. One leader is on record for rebuking a woman in his congregation, who was checking out what he was saying with what the Bible in front of her stated.

The master of biblical misquotation, of course, is Satan himself. In his third assault of temptation, the devil unsuccessfully tried to divert Jesus from His core redemptive mission, inviting Him to test the faithfulness of His Father. Jesus saw through the ruse. Let's be aware that the Bible has been used to justify all kinds of terrible events in history, from the Crusades to apartheid. And surely not an hour goes by without a text being used to control, hurt or manipulate. When someone says, 'The Bible says', let's consider the context of their quotation, as well as the burden of what the Bible says overall, lest we too take a leap that God never wanted us to take. It's an old saying, but a scripture taken out of context is a pretext.

Prayer: Your Word is a sharp sword, Lord. Help me to use it wisely. Amen.

a scripture
taken out of
context is
a pretext

Protection and yet mystery

Read:
Psalm 34:1–22
Hebrews 1:14

FOCUS

'The angel of the LORD encamps around those who fear him, and he delivers them.'
(Psa. 34:7)

Reflecting on the truth that angelic beings protect those who love God, I can struggle. As I write today, a friend is watching her father die from the effects of Covid. The obvious question is – where is the protection for that dear man? And I have heard soundly authenticated stories of Christians who experienced angelic intervention when they were under attack from marauding terrorists intent on murdering them because of their love for Christ. But then, just this week, news came from Nigeria that hundreds of Christians had been brutally slaughtered by fanatical Islamists. Again, were the angels caught off guard?

But then I looked at the preface to this psalm, which shows us the context of its writing. David was living through one of the most terrifying seasons of his life. On the run from murderous Saul, he ended up in Gath, the place where he had killed Goliath. But there he faced renewed danger from the king, Achish, (referred to as Abimelek in the introduction to this psalm), and had to pretend that he was insane in order to avoid capture and death (1 Sam 21:10–15). David's life was in total upheaval, yet in the midst of those trials, he affirms angelic protection. Even when the going is hard and having faith calls us to embrace mystery, let's be aware an unseen battle is raging. We have probably been spared much because of the ministry of angels sent to those who will inherit salvation – us, by the grace of God and through the rescuing work of Jesus.

an unseen battle is raging

Prayer: Father, surely many things occur unseen by me. Thank you for grace that I'm not aware of, but surrounds me, nevertheless. Amen.

Expectation and Wonder

Advent with Waverley Abbey Trust

Spark up the countdown as we reinvent adventing.
Join us for events to raise your wonder and build your
expectation. Dare to believe again this year.

Discover events, inspiration, group resources and creative
spaces to help you reflect on advent.

 C2C Advent: Journey to Christmas

 C2C Advent: Unexpected Jesus

 Advent Together

Journeying together through advent

waverleyabbeyresources.org/advent-2021

Angelic missions

Read:
2 Kings 6:8–23
Psalm 34:1–22

....

FOCUS

'Then the LORD opened the servant's eyes, and he looked and saw the hills full of horses and chariots of fire all around Elisha.' (2 Kings 6:17)

God is revealed in the book of Psalms as the supreme commander of the angelic host, and there are many biblical accounts we could look at to further consider this truth. Over the next three days, we will concentrate on just three of them. Psalm 34:7 gives us a picture of encamped angels and, as a further example of this, most commentators point to Elisha's experience when under attack from the Aramean army. Elisha's servant was quite unaware of the presence of angelic warriors until Elisha prayed his eyes would be open to see them. I love the words of comfort and encouragement found here: 'Don't be afraid... Those who are with us are more than those who are with them' (2 Kings 6:16).

Nowhere in Scripture are we encouraged to seek angels out, however, or to be hungry to encounter them, as I have said. We are called to worship Jesus and pursue His presence, not a substitute. That said, we do need to look at life through the eyes of faith, especially when challenges mount up. We're not called to deny the problems we face – that's not faith, it's unreality. But in the midst of those challenges and the unseen warfare, we declare there is a God, and He can intervene, strengthen, speak and protect. We are not left to our own resources. Not only are angels at work around us, but the Holy Spirit empowers us from within – and that always puts us in the majority, whatever our circumstances. Or to put it another way, if God be for us, who can be against us?

He can intervene

Prayer: Give me eyes of faith, Lord. Amen.

Led into the eye of the storm

A fellow student at the Bible College that I attended, Joy Bath was quiet, kind and beautiful, a warm smile usually on her face. A qualified nurse, Joy was preparing for the mission field in Zimbabwe. Back then, little was known about the Aids virus, and she contracted it while working in the delivery room of a hospital. Wearing sandals for a birth, contaminated blood infiltrated a graze on her foot. Joy knew there were serious risks in her work, but she felt such a strong call from God to serve people and share the good news of Jesus. She was led directly into the eye of a storm; she died in faith at the age of 44.

As we read of the heavenly hosts worshipping their captain, we also see how the angel of the Lord not only delivered the apostles from prison in a supernatural jailbreak, but then commanded them to go right back to the Temple courts to declare the gospel message. Experiencing the jailbreak must have been such a relief, but now God was calling them to be brave again in the face of danger. This was no vague threat. Some would seek to bring the death penalty against them, and they did end up being flogged – most likely the terrible 39 lashes. Despite being warned not to, they carried on preaching.

The apostles prized obedience over comfort and personal safety. Joy Bath quietly served without fuss, and she stands in the distinguished line of the glorious faithful. If the time comes for us to be tested, may we be found faithful too.

Prayer: When You lead me into trouble and stress rather than away from it, may I keep in step, Father. Amen.

Read:
Psalm 148:1–14
Acts 5:17–42

FOCUS
'Praise him, all his angels; praise him, all his heavenly hosts.' (Psa. 148:2)

God was calling them to be brave again

Read:
Psalm 103:1–22
Acts 12:1–17

The angels know that we're weak

Have you ever listened to a preacher boldly declaring they know what God is saying during a current season, and felt yourself to be very weak in faith, in comparison? Often we preachers are loud with our headlines of breakthrough and victory, but are quieter about the back stories of struggle, doubt and bewilderment. That's why I love Scripture, because it is so honest. Those armies of angels – they 'obey his word' (Psa. 103:20). We humans can be a little slower in our response. The episode described in Acts 12 always fills me with hope, because Peter is dull in his response to yet another jailbreaking angel. This heavenly being has to tell him to get dressed and, even as he goes out of the door, Peter thinks he is just dreaming. Finally he 'came to himself' and then has major trouble as he tries to get into a prayer meeting, called to request his release. Those inside don't believe the man frantically knocking at the door is Peter. We are weak. God is strong – and patient with it.

To ponder: Do you view God as patient? Can you think of a season in your life when He showed special patience towards you?

Weekend

I love Scripture

The right-handed God

As we turn to the picture of God's right hand, a very frequent image in the book of Psalms, I confess I have a specific personal interest in this aspect of His character. More about that later. Broadly speaking, the concept of being at the Lord's right hand speaks of being set in a place of honour. And so our Lord Jesus, having completed His work of atoning sacrifice, is now seated at the right hand of the Father. Conversely, at the final judgment, the sheep of God's flock are found at His right hand, while the so-called goats are at the left. We'll explore this image at a deeper level over the next week or so, but for now, let's know that, because of Christ, because of grace, because of God's love, we are now found in a place of honour in God's family. Many of us don't feel like that; we fret that perhaps we have worn God's patience thin with our acts of rebellion; that He rolls His eyes when we offer our sleepy prayers; that His response to our worship is a snort of disdain. As I've frequently said, it can be easier to believe that God loves the world, rather than believe He is utterly filled with love towards us as individuals. Nor is that honour reserved for the future, when we see Jesus face to face: it is how God sees us and feels towards us now. 'I know my place' is a statement often made by someone made to feel inferior and dejected. Today, know your place – it is at His right hand.

Prayer: Your sacrifice for me places me at Your right hand, Lord. I am loved, honoured, favoured, now. Thank you. Amen.

Read:
Psalm 98:1–9
Matthew 25:31–46

FOCUS

'His right hand and his holy arm have worked salvation for him.' (Psa. 98:1)

our Lord Jesus … is now seated at the right hand of the Father

His hand upon me – and you

....

FOCUS

'Even there your hand will guide me, your right hand will hold me fast.'
(Psa. 139:10)

I want to labour the point I made yesterday, and for good reason. A pastor for over forty years now, I constantly meet Christians who feel nervous and apprehensive about their relationship with God. They believe in God's grace, but don't rest in it. They can quote verses from the Bible about His forgiveness and cleansing, but still live with their heads down and their hearts heavy, seemingly paralysed because of past or present sins. Again, they are convinced about God's love generally, but not particularly – for them. The psalmist repeatedly makes the point that God's right hand of favour and honour are upon *him*. And then when we look beyond the book of Psalms, we see the apostle Paul celebrating the truth of the Son of God, who 'loved *me* and gave himself for *me*' (Gal. 2:20, italics mine). Remember, this was the man who had inflicted such horrendous pain upon the Early Church as a persecutor. When we read Paul's writings in the New Testament, we see him looking back on his own horrible history with deep regret, even calling himself 'the worst of sinners' at one point (1 Tim. 1:15). He never tries to excuse himself for the terrible things he'd done, including his approval of the slaughter of believers (Acts 8:1). But he gave us a third of the New Testament, and unpacked the treasures of grace for us. He lived convinced that whatever was past, God's right hand was upon him in the present and forever. May the same be true for us.

'loved *me* and gave himself for *me*'

Prayer: When I am tempted to look back in regret and shame, help me to look further back, at what You have done to redeem me, Lord Jesus. Amen.

The right-handed God we thirst for

Read:
Psalm 63:1–11
Matthew 5:1–10

FOCUS

'I cling to you; your right hand upholds me.' (Psa. 63:8)

Regular readers of *Life Every Day* will know that Kay and I frequently lead tours to the Holy Land and Jordan. No matter how many times we return, we so love being in the landscape of the Bible. Our tour guides are amazing, and not only share their wealth of information with us, but look out for our wellbeing too. One of the most frequent announcements – often multiple times in a day – is the call to drink water, because the climate presents significant risks of dehydration. That helps me appreciate the weary cry of the psalmist, who is like a bewildered trekker in the desert, desperately looking for water.

David uses this picture to illustrate his urgent thirst for God. For him, God is no optional extra, no helpful addition or emergency call-out person – David is parched in his desire for God. As I read his words, and his confession that in his seeking and searching, the right hand of God 'upholds' and sustains him, I confess there have been seasons when I have not had much of a thirst for God myself. Instead, my desires have been fixated on lesser, temporal things. And sometimes, despite thirstiness for God – when He seems absent, or silent – I have simply meandered on regardless, rather than seeking him urgently. But when we seek Him, we will be upheld by Him. As we read Jesus' words about those who hunger and thirst for righteousness, let's ask the Lord to give us a greater hunger and thirst for Him. God waits to be wanted.

Prayer: Father, I want to be among those who are desperate for You, who seek You with their whole hearts. Amen.

when we seek Him, we will be upheld by Him

His mighty hand

....

FOCUS

'Your arm is endowed with power; your hand is strong, your right hand exalted.'
(Psa. 89:13)

Life has a way of diminishing our vision of the mightiness and stunning power of God. Disappointment, lingering illness and seemingly unheard prayers all edge us into a kind of amnesia. We still vaguely believe that God has incredible power – He brought creation into being by just speaking words of command – but while we might sing about his power on Sunday mornings, we struggled to connect that truth to our Monday morning difficulties. But His strength matters. The expression, 'the right hand of God' speaks not only of His heart to place us in a situation of honour, but also of His mighty power. In this psalm, God's power is emphasised in that He alone can command the turbulent waves of the sea, which helps us to understand why Jesus walked on water. That was not just an impressive show, but a display of divine authority and power, as was His calming of the storm. And the psalmist speaks of God's power over that of Egypt – 'Rahab' was a popular nickname for that nation – and elsewhere, even over the mighty Babylon (Psa. 87:4).

I can think of a number of areas in my own life that I seldom pray about because they present what seems like an insurmountable challenge. Today, in affirming God's mighty power, I am going to bring those needs before the Lord once more. While I cannot be assured of what God *will* do, I can affirm what He *can* do. Why not join me as you consider your own challenges? God is able.

He alone can command the turbulent waves

Prayer: Lord of the waves, help me to translate what I believe about Your power into my heart and mind, when storms roll in. Amen.

His gentle right hand

Incredible power and gentleness don't usually go together; when humans gain power, they usually abuse and oppress others. And that, sadly, can also be true of Christian leaders, who can use Scripture and the idea of God to bully and control. Buried in Psalm 18, and lost in many translations, is a word best translated as 'gentleness', a word only used here in the Bible to describe God. Commentators throughout the centuries have wrestled with this statement: how does the gentleness of God make anyone great? While we can't be certain, we do know that the Bible reveals our God as gentle, as does the description of His Son, Jesus. Jesus invites us to come to Him because, as He says, 'I am gentle and humble in heart, and you will find rest for your souls' (Matt. 11:29). And the apostle Paul spoke of the 'humility and gentleness of Christ' (2 Cor. 10:1). Surely all of us have experienced the untiring patience of God, who is slow to anger. As the hymn, 'Praise, my soul, the King of heaven', (based on Psalm 103) says:

'Father-like he tends and spares us. Well our feeble frame He knows. In his arms He gently bears us. Rescues us from all our foes...'

This God has the power to crumple planets in His hand, and yet He knows us utterly, loves us totally, and will love us always. Let's live in the knowledge of His gentle care, and be like Him, allowing the fruit of the Spirit, which includes gentleness, to blossom in our lives and relationships.

Prayer: The fruit of Your work in us includes gentleness, Holy Spirit. May I be gentle, especially when I am frustrated. Amen.

Read:
Psalm 18:1–35
Psalm 103:1–22

....

FOCUS

'You have given me the shield of your salvation, and your right hand supported me, and your gentleness made me great.'
(Psa. 18:35, ESV)

God has the power to crumple planets in His hand

Other Jeff Lucas Titles

Specks and Planks

This collection of stories by Jeff will amuse, challenge and – when tempted to display speck-hunting and plank-protruding behaviour – motivate all of us to show more kindness and be less swift to judge.

Faith in the Fog

This books is surprisingly uplifting and gives the reader permission to doubt, to make mistakes and to question – after all that is what Peter did. Most Christians live out their faith in times of fog but Jesus is the light that we can focus on.

It's a Dog's Life

Stories showing the brighter side of life and encouraging us that God can redeem our mistakes. Jeff Lucas is back with another collection of humorous and heart-warming stories from his life and travels as a pastor.

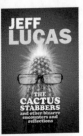

The Cactus Stabbers

Jeff looks at life through his realistic, yet optimistic, lenses. Each chapter tells a different story but all have one thing in common, pondering human nature. Jeff invites us to step back and take a look at our own lives as he shares from his life too.

There are no Ordinary People

This refreshingly honest book, filled with Jeff's brilliant combination of thought-provoking observations, wisdom and humour, explores what it means to be an everyday hero. Two thousand years ago lived a seemingly ordinary man called Barnabas. He played an absolutely vital role in the beginnings of the Early Church, but finding a book about Barnabas can be very difficult until now...

There are no Strong People

Is it possible to be hugely blessed by God – and still make a mess of your life? In this provocative, honest book, Jeff Lucas explores some vital principles for living life well. Based on the life of the Bible's infamous Samson, this book asks its readers to think, re-evaluate and dig deeper.

Weekend

Strengthened by His right hand

It's ironic really. When life is hard, the pressure is on and our faith is low, we tend to neglect prayer. We're too tired to bother, we're quietly frustrated with God because of our circumstances, or perhaps we feel there's no point. But spending time with God can have a very tangible effect upon us; our mood and our perspective can shift. David wrote Psalm 60 during a time of military defeat, when his spirits were very low. The first three verses of the psalm vividly describe his despair. But as his lament continues, there is a shift, and the downcast David cries out 'Save us and help us with your right hand, that those you love may be delivered' (Psa. 60:5). Look how the psalm ends: 'With God we will gain the victory, and he will trample down our enemies' (v12). God chooses to use prayer to strengthen us, which is why we're commanded to pray during temptation. When we struggle, let's not drift away or draw back. Let's draw near, and find strength in time of need.

To ponder: Have you experienced being strengthened through prayer?

God chooses to use prayer
to strengthen us

He delivers with His right hand

Read:
Psalm 60:1–5
Job 7:7–21

FOCUS

'Save us and help us with your right hand, that those you love may be delivered.' (Psa. 60:5).

Talking with a dear friend yesterday, I did my best to help as he shared his struggles with faith. Living through long months of anxiety and fear coupled with sickness, he finds the idea that God intervenes and answers prayer difficult. His spiritual life has ground to a halt, and these days the only prayers he can offer are filled with muttering and anger. These, by the way, are valid prayers; God wants us to express how we feel to Him, and the whole book of Psalms vividly illustrates this.

As I listened to him pouring out his soul, keen not to offer hollow slogans in response, I realised that I also so often talk about doubt, disappointment and the angst that can come in the journey of faith. I can drift into spending more time defending God, and forget to affirm the many times when He has intervened and answered prayer remarkably. Too much time in that negative way of thinking can edge us into a place where we talk to God woodenly, out of duty and obligation, but with very little expectation of any response – and that's not where I want to be. Prayer with that mindset deteriorates into cold religious obligation.

As once again the psalmist speaks of God's right hand, he cries out to God to deliver him, and he obviously anticipates some response. It's not easy to mingle expectation with an ability to trust in the midst of mystery and even disappointment, but it's the delicate balance that I want in my faith walk, and in yours too.

Prayer: Be my vision, Lord, the source of my strength and hope today. Amen.

God wants us to express how we feel to Him

Eternity at His right hand

....

FOCUS

'You will fill me with joy in your presence, with eternal pleasures at your right hand.'
(Psa. 16:11).

Earlier we saw that the Coronavirus pandemic brought the reality of death much closer to us, as daily we heard dark statistics, and then people we knew fell ill or even succumbed to the dreaded virus. I'd like to return to the truth that the power of death is beaten today. As we hear David's words (Peter ascribes these words to David in his preaching in Acts), we are not just affirming that life after death will be wonderful for those in Christ. Rather, David is perhaps being prophetic, letting us know that the joy of knowing Christ in the here and now will continue uninterrupted through death. While death creates grief and sorrow in the separation it brings, and it is still 'the last enemy', yet, through Jesus' death and resurrection, our partnership and friendship with Him will not be fractured by death, but will continue throughout eternity.

It's been said that eternity is in flight, right now. As believers, we don't have to wait until we cross the boundary line between life and death to experience God's closeness and the blessing of being at His right hand. Today, by faith, we know that He is with us. If our circumstances are harrowing, yet we are not abandoned. German theologian and pastor Dietrich Bonhoeffer experienced such a strong sense of the presence and comfort of God while incarcerated, awaiting execution. Today, even in turmoil, we are not alone. May you know the reality of Him being with You, not just as a theory, but as a reality, today.

we are not
abandoned

Prayer: Here, now, today, You are mine, and always will be. I praise You, heavenly Father. Amen.

His right hand of justice

istening to an exhausted, distraught doctor during the Covid crisis, my heart sank as she reported receiving abusive messages – sometimes up to thirty each day. Most disappointing were the so-called 'trolls' who said they were going to refuse to follow the lockdown rules and guidelines, and they didn't care if people died as a result. Their blatant self-centredness shocked me. But then I wondered if I am guilty of more subtle forms of selfish living. When I don't think too hard about the sources that I buy from: are workers being oppressed? When I ignore my responsibilities as a tenant of this planet, and not its owner, does the planet suffer? How can I reflect God's heart for justice, when my spending is all about a preoccupation with my own needs and a refusal to respond to the poor?

The Bible is clear that the God of all power is passionately concerned about the needs of those we view as weak and unimportant. As we read the unusual wording, 'your right hand is filled with righteousness', (an image repeated in Psalm 91), we see the key word. 'Righteousness' speaks of things being done rightly: in relationships, in business, in all of life. And we're told to make seeking the kingdom of God and His righteousness our top priority. God cares, and when we care as well, we point the world to His powerful yet tender heart. There are small steps we can take to align ourselves with the God who loves justice. What steps might you take?

Prayer: You love Your world and all in it, Lord. Show me how to reflect that love and Your heart for justice for all. Amen.

Read:
Psalm 48:1–14,
Psalm 98:1

FOCUS

'Your praise reaches to the ends of the earth; your right hand is filled with righteousness.'
(Psa. 48:10).

God cares

His hand, His arm, His face

Read:
Psalm 44:1–7
Psalm 89:13–15

....

FOCUS

'It was your right hand, your arm, and the light of your face, for you loved them.'
(Psa. 44:3)

The dating of this psalm is hotly disputed, and the exact circumstances in which it was written unknown, but what we do know is Israel had experienced defeat at the hands of an unnamed enemy. In that place, the psalmist looks back at what God had done in history, in both the distant and recent past. Scan the Old Testament and you'll see God frequently instructed His people to build monuments, pillars, and stones to help them recall His mighty acts, because He knows how easily we forget.

Twice today, I had the opportunity to share an amazing intervention from the Lord that happened when my father passed away. That episode happened 25 years ago, but as I recalled the incident, my faith was strengthened today by what happened in yesteryear. Then notice the beautifully vivid picture that the psalm evokes of the God whose 'right hand and arm' helps, and who also aids us by 'the light of his face'. These word pictures remind us of the personhood of God. We are not just sustained or strengthened by a great force, 'may the force be with you', but by a Father. We don't just go to God as the source of blessing, but to Him personally, in a relationship of love and affection.

We touched on this earlier, but I don't just want to ask God for things: not even for His help, although we declare that God has helped us, and will help us. I want to seek His face, and knows the blesser more deeply. This is not about hungering for the blessing, but Him who bestows it.

a relationship of love and affection

Prayer: I seek You Lord, Your face as well as Your hand. Amen.

His right hand on the darkest of days

Read:
Psalm 118:1–29
Mark 14:12–26

FOCUS

'The LORD's right hand has done mighty things! The LORD's right hand is lifted high; the LORD's right hand has done mighty things!'
(Psa. 118:15–16)

Come with me to the upper room, where Jesus shared that last supper with His friends and disciples, before going out to face the awful experiences of Gethsemane and Calvary. Before going to face agonising death, Jesus sang a hymn with His closest circle, and we almost certainly know what they sang. It was customary to share the Hallel hymn (Psa. 113–118) during the Passover meal, which includes these wonderful words about God's right hand. Notice the powerful words of hope as the cross loomed closer: 'I will not die but live, and will proclaim what the LORD has done' (v17). And then, 'The stone the builders rejected has become the cornerstone; the LORD has done this, and it is marvellous in our eyes' (vv22–23). Knowing that He was utterly committed to the Father's will, whatever the cost, on that darkest of evenings, Jesus was able to declare the final words of the hymn: 'Give thanks to the LORD, for he is good; his love endures forever' (v29). Surely feeling weak, Jesus leaned hard on the Father's right hand and arm.

How amazing that Jesus took these words of hope upon His lips, words that so poignantly spoke into His circumstances. Often when something wonderful happens, we excitedly say God is good, but then when pain, grief or death approaches, we might not be so sure. But whatever our circumstances, we affirm that God's right hand is strong, and that He is good – yes, all the time. And nothing on earth can change that!

Prayer: You are good, Lord, and Your love endures forever. Amen.

'Give thanks to the LORD, for he is good'

When His hand seems withdrawn

We're about to move on from this picture of the 'right-handed' God, but before we do, authenticity requires that I share the psalmist's experience when he felt that 'God's right hand' was nowhere to be seen in his life. In this psalm, the question is asked, 'Why do you hold back your hand, your right hand? (Psa. 74:11). Yesterday we saw that Jesus went to the cross affirming the goodness of His Father. But we know that, on the cross, He experienced something of the agony of abandonment as He cried, 'My God, my God, why have you forsaken me?'

In recent times, we have all lived through circumstances where many were asking God to intervene. Yet, at a global level with the pandemic, we did not see deliverance come quite as we would have all hoped. At times when we feel that God has power, but He is not using it in a way we would choose, we can take a leaf out of the psalmist's book, and be honest with our feelings of frustration. God knows what's in our hearts anyway.

To ponder: Are you comfortable with being honest about your feelings to God?

the goodness of His Father

Redeemer: taking responsibility

Read:
Psalm 19:1–14
Ruth 4:1–12

FOCUS

'May these words of my mouth and this meditation of my heart be pleasing in your sight, LORD, my Rock and my Redeemer.'
(Psa. 19:14)

Recently, I've been reflecting on what it takes to be a good friend. Authentic kingdom friendships go far beyond being able to laugh together. Surely God wants us to enjoy relationships that are more substantial than simply enjoying each other's company. As we read that God is our redeemer, we discover something about what it means to be a real friend. The word 'redeemer' here is the Hebrew word *goel*, which was used to describe someone's closest relative, normally a brother. The family *goel* carried heavy responsibilities. We see this powerfully illustrated in the story of Ruth and Boaz. If the family land or property was threatened by debt, the *goel* was expected to step up and buy it. If someone in the family became destitute and sold themselves into slavery, the *goel* would be called upon to buy their freedom. The key word to describe this role is *responsibility*. I think that's what happens in true friendship; people take responsibility for each other; to help, confront, comfort and even rescue. Even today, I found myself in the awkward position of having to confront a friend because I love him; faithfulness demands I take responsibility. Godly friendship has such an element to it. We'll consider how God is a friend 'who is closer than a brother' to us tomorrow, in His work as the great *goel* or redeemer, but before we move forward, let's ask: have we built such friendships, where we share a sense a mutual responsibility for those we love?

Prayer: I want friendships of depth, where mutual responsibility for each is felt and carried. Help me to build relationships like that, Father. Amen.

God wants us to enjoy relationships

God took responsibility for us

....

FOCUS

*'They remembered
that God was their
Rock, that God Most
High was their
Redeemer.'*
(Psa. 78:35)

Yesterday we saw that the redeemer, the *goel* in a family carried responsibility both for rescue and for restoration – for putting things back as they should be. And that's what our God has done for us. The word is used nearly 150 times in the Old Testament, and most references speak about God 'redeeming' His people from the oppressive clutches of Egypt and then leading them to the Promised Land. A people who had been harshly enslaved were not just rescued in a great evacuation across the Red Sea, but were taken to a land 'flowing with milk and honey'. Christ redeemed us from 'the curse of the law' (Gal. 3:13), from 'all wickedness" (Titus 2:14), and from 'sins committed' (Heb. 9:15). But redeeming doesn't just save us *from* something; we are saved *to* a life that is far more satisfying and beautiful than anything we had before we came to Christ. And all this happened because God took responsibility for us.

In the biblical use of the word redeemer, the person who was redeemed was very aware of the hopelessness of their situation; they were helpless, unable to get out from under that mountain of debt, bound by the shackles of slavery and powerless to do anything to change their lot. It was only when the redeemer arrived that everything changed for the good. Today, let's rest fully in God's redeeming work, knowing there was and is nothing we could do to save ourselves. Let's worship and give thanks, and live the life for which God has rescued us.

God took
responsibility
for us

Prayer: Nothing in my hand did I bring, or can I bring, to save myself. You rescued and redeemed me, to live with and for You. Amen.

He is the redeemer: a price paid

The picture of God as redeemer in the Old Testament is picked up in the New Testament, as we saw yesterday. The word is used 19 times in the New Testament, and there the aspect of the *goel* paying a price is emphasised. And what a price was paid, as Jesus did salvation's work by laying down His life for us (Heb. 9:12). The writer to the Hebrews contrasts the sacrifices of animals under the law with the freewill sacrifice of Christ. Those animals had no choice in the matter; obviously, they were used in the ceremonies without consent, but Jesus freely gave Himself for us. The apostle Peter celebrates this great sacrifice of love in his first epistle (1 Pet.1:18–21), using the picture of the Passover lamb to illustrate that we have been redeemed with nothing less than the precious blood of Christ, a lamb without blemish or defect' (1 Pet. 1:19).

Today, I don't want to rush to a personal life application for us, but rather invite you to join with me in pondering this wonderful characteristic of our God. We've already seen that He took total responsibility for our salvation, but He did so, not out of obligation, but willingly, out of love. Let's take time today to offer grateful worship, which involves thanksgiving, praise, but also the offering of our own lives once again to His purposes and service. He has given Himself totally to and for us; let's respond in the same way, freely offering ourselves to Him without reservation.

Prayer: May I truly be able to say, Lord Jesus: whatever You say, I will do it. Amen.

Read:
Hebrews 9:11–14
Psalm 130:1–8

....

FOCUS

'He did not enter by means of the blood of goats and calves... he entered the Most Holy Place once for all by his own blood ... obtaining eternal redemption.'
(Heb. 9:12).

He took total responsibility for our salvation

Invest in your mental health and wellbeing

Learn online, at your own pace, and gain greater knowledge to better understand yourself and others.

Would you like to feel better equipped at supporting friends or family through difficult times? Perhaps you'd like some guidance to understand your own mental health or wellbeing challenges.

Whether you're going through a blip, or supporting somebody who is, these courses will help you understand how and why some people are affected in these areas. Through the Insight learning platform, you'll discover the value of a healthy mindset and ways to navigate challenges.

Insight into Anxiety

Anxiety affects many people today. Explore key issues with anxiety, and skills and strategies to manage and overcome it. This course offers insight for those who want to help others, as well as those who face issues with anxiety themselves.

Insight into Self-Esteem

This 4 session course will lead you through an exploration of the importance of self esteem and how as Christians it is rooted in our relationship with God.

To find out more about our Insight courses please visit

waverleyabbeyresources.org/insight

He redeemed us, so don't look back

....

FOCUS

'For you know that it was not with perishable things such as silver or gold that you were redeemed from the empty way of life handed down to you.' (1 Pet. 1:18).

The thought surfaced at the end of a day when I had felt particularly discouraged. An unkind email had landed in my inbox, containing scathing, critical language from someone that I actually thought of as a friend. Christians were fighting on Facebook, and I felt bone weary. The unthinkable idea occurred – what if I had never become a Christian so many years ago? Discipleship demands effort, sacrifice, alertness. Would my life had been more carefree and relaxed if I'd not made the choice to become a follower of Jesus? But that idea was quickly filed under the heading of what the Bible describes as 'futile' thinking. The truth that God redeems shows us there was something from which we needed to be redeemed, as we've seen. And Peter, knowing that Jesus had promised him a martyr's death, so he would lose everything for the cause of Christ, reminds his readers – and you and me – that we were rescued from an 'empty way of life'. It didn't take me long to acknowledge that my decision to journey with Jesus was absolutely the best choice I've ever made.

Sometimes, especially when we feel like we're in a spiritual wilderness, looking back to Egypt is a temptation. How quickly we forget the oppression and hopelessness that we experienced there, as God's people in the Exodus forgot. Today, let's not look back except with thanksgiving, and look forward and upward. Nothing that we left for Christ was worth having.

Jesus was absolutely the best choice I've ever made

Prayer: When empty living disguises itself as an attractive option, help me to see through the deception, and follow You, all the way home, Jesus. Amen.

The redeemer: God of the turnaround

Read:
2 Samuel 11:1–27
Matthew 1:1–16

FOCUS

'After... mourning was over, David had her brought to his house, and she became his wife and bore him a son. But the thing David had done displeased the LORD.' (2 Sam 11:27)

Before we move on from considering God as the redeemer, I'd like to offer an observation that has repeatedly been confirmed over the years. God is the redeemer – the One who turns things around – in many situations for which He bears no responsibility: He didn't make them happen. We see that in the life of David, who wrote so many of the psalms. It was obviously not God's plan that David committed adultery and then arranged for the death of Bathsheba's husband Uriah, a man of true loyalty and integrity. This act by David was conspiracy to murder, and judgment followed. But it was out of the genealogical line forged by David and Bathsheba that Solomon came, that famously wise king. And then, perhaps staggeringly, fast forward from that initially dreadful union of David and Bathsheba and we find the birth of Jesus. As a pastor, I have seen countless examples of God redeeming terrible situations and turning ashes into gold. I've watched as people who suffered long term painful illnesses matured in their faith as a result of their difficult journey. I've seen terrible, foolish decisions repented of, and then better days following because God turned what the enemy meant for evil to His good purposes. That doesn't mean that we should blunder into sin, confident that God will untangle and redeem the mess we've made, but it does mean we have a mighty God who can restore and redeem when we turn to Him. He is the God of the turnaround!

Prayer: I thank you that you can take even my failures and redeem them, Father. My redeemer lives. Amen.

turning ashes into gold

God delighted and dancing

Kay's suggestion that we take dancing lessons didn't turn out well. I'd love to be able to whisk her around the dance floor with smooth, apparently effortless moves, but it just isn't going to happen. My feet don't seem to be connected to my brain, and when some connection is established, it's usually with a three-second delay, which doesn't help coordination. A dancer I will never be. But I'm glad to report that, in a sense, God is dancer. Once again the psalmist declares God's delight in him. In Zephaniah, an otherwise fairly gloomy book about doom and judgment, God offers hope as He promises to delight in His people, and rejoice over them with singing. A careful look at the Hebrew of that verse suggests God 'spinning around under violent emotion', a singing, dancing God. I'm reminded of the picture of the Father in the prodigal son story, throwing decorum aside and dashing out to fold his returning (and somewhat smelly) son into his arms. What a wonderful God we serve!

To ponder: How do you respond to the imagery of a singing, dancing God – who sighs and dances … over you?

Weekend

God offers hope

The delighted bridegroom God

Read:
Psalm 18:1–19
Isaiah 62:1–5

FOCUS

'He brought me out into a spacious place; he rescued me because he delighted in me.' (Psa. 18:19).

Recently Kay and I have spent some time reflecting on the journey we have taken together. When we got married back in 1978, we had little in the way of financial resources. Scratch that. We were broke. We remember hoping and praying people would give us money on our wedding day, rather than items for our home, because we needed some cash to go on honeymoon. Our honeymoon was spent firstly in my grandmother's house (we're not sure where she went while we were there for a week!), and then we stayed at a guest house in Wales – where the owner saw that we were so broke, he cut the bill in half and gave us that money as a wedding gift! Despite our poverty, though, we were just so delighted to be married. I was also amazed my beautiful wife had agreed to marry me – and the amazement continues! David speaks about God delighting in him – so effusive is his language that some commentators suggest he must have been prophetically describing the Father's delight in the Son. Whether or not this is true, Isaiah tells us God delights in us like a thrilled bridegroom over his bride.

When we think of God in His relationship to us personally, do we tend to view Him as being thrilled to know us and be with us, or have we a tendency to think perhaps He is less than pleased? We celebrated the truth of this yesterday, but it's worth revisiting. Today, God delights ... in you, like a bridegroom, overjoyed on his wedding day.

Prayer: These portraits of Your delight can shape my view of You, Lord. By Your Spirit, may I stand more confidently in Your Fatherly care. Amen.

God delights in us

What especially delights God?

Read:
Psalm 18:20–50
Psalm 149:1–9

FOCUS

*'The LORD has dealt
with me according
to my righteousness;
according to the
cleanness of my
hands he has
rewarded me.'*
(Psa. 18:20)

As we return to Psalm 18, David further unpacks what it is God especially delights in. Bear in mind David was far from perfect, and perhaps he was wrong in his profession of his own righteousness here. Nevertheless, with all his flaws, he is twice described as a man after God's heart (1 Sam. 13:14, Acts 13:22) and his intentions to walk in holiness pleased God, even though there were frequent, significant falls. David's failures included lying; serving as a mercenary for Israel's old enemy, the Philistines; over-focusing on numbers and his own strength rather than relying on God; failing to have the Ark of the Lord carried properly; failure as a father to discipline his rapist son Amnon; and the adultery and conspiracy to murder that I mentioned earlier. Quite a lengthy list of significant faults!

But in his favour, he hungered for God, shown by the 73 psalms of worship attributed to him, plus possibly more written anonymously. He persisted in bringing the Ark home to Jerusalem, and provided a new tabernacle for it. He appointed worship musicians and singers as full-time posts, and planned for resources for his son, Solomon, to build the Temple. He never drifted into idolatry, unlike most of the kings of Israel and Judah.

God isn't looking for perfection, but He delights in those who relentlessly pursue Him. Don't be spiritually paralysed when you fail. Get up, and continue in your pursuit of God, and be a person after God's own heart.

a man after
God's heart

Prayer: May my fragility never discourage me from following You, faithful Lord Jesus. Amen.

Delight versus betrayal

Earlier, I mentioned some of the challenges of the Christian life, especially leadership. Looking back over four decades of ministry, I have found it especially hard to deal with betrayal. I can think of some people who were given significant opportunities by my colleagues and me. They responded with delight and gratitude, but when power came their way, they used their platforms to hurt and criticise those of us who had provided those platforms. That was tough to swallow, and I confess that I occasionally lapse into a less than forgiving attitude. I don't wish a plague of boils upon them, but an irksome wart or two might be useful...

Then there are those who have not only been faithful, but have truly celebrated with me when blessing and opportunity have come my way. A genuine friend is able to cheer us on in success, as well as comfort us in failure. As David bewails his lot in Psalm 35, because he has been betrayed and those he thought of as friends are gloating over his struggles, he celebrates the God who delights in his wellbeing. The God we serve is thrilled when we do well. Let's emulate Him in our relationships, and celebrate with those who don't only do well, but who are even more successful than we are. Envy is ugly and reveals deep-seated self-centredness. So let's rejoice with those who rejoice. That way we'll reflect the character of the God who delights in our wellbeing – and we'll bless our friends as we do.

Prayer: Give me grace to know the joy of celebrating with those who do better than me, Lord. Amen.

Read:
Psalm 35
Romans 12:15

....

FOCUS

'May those who delight in my vindication shout for joy and gladness; may they always say, "The LORD be exalted, who delights in the well-being of his servant."'
(Psa. 35:27)

the God who delights in his wellbeing

Shepherd

....

FOCUS

'The LORD is my shepherd, I lack nothing.' (Psa. 23:1)

I'd like to spend the final few days in our journey in considering the characteristics of God in the book of Psalms by looking at the best known psalm of them all: the much loved Psalm 23. But our familiarity with these words can cause us to miss some of their depth and beauty. The statement, 'The LORD is my shepherd' speaks both of need and power. It's not surprising that we humans are often described in Scripture as being like sheep. I learnt a lot about the habits of sheep in the Middle East at this time from Philip Keller's book, A Shepherd Looks at Psalm 23. Sheep aren't that bright, tend to be timid and stubborn, frequently meander off and get themselves into real problems. Sound familiar? Sheep can be high maintenance – it's been said that more than any other class of livestock at that time, they required meticulous care and endless attention. That picture brings human pride crashing down to earth, because with all of our ingenuity and brilliance, we still need help.

But help is available, and the helper is the Lord Himself. The welfare of the sheep is so dependent on the character and ability of the shepherd – a neglectful shepherd will lead to a weak, thin flock, diseased and tormented by parasites. But in our case, God, who spoke the universe into being with just a word – He has pledged to care for us. We confess our need, but we don't stop there. We also affirm the Mighty One is with us and for us.

the helper
is the Lord
Himself

Prayer: You, Lord, maker of heaven and earth and all that there is: You are my shepherd. Amen.

Content in His care

The preacher was really excited. He picked up his Bible in his bejewelled hand, and slammed it down onto the pulpit, a gesture suggesting he was about to make an absolute statement, one beyond contradiction. 'Because the Bible tells me that God is my shepherd, it then promises that I will never be wanting for anything. Lack and poverty are impossible for me, if I just trust Him!' He jabbed a finger at the adoring congregation. 'What about you – are you going to a accept lack and need when the good shepherd promises you plenty?'

The sermon was carefully presented and delivered with passion – and demonstrated how easily Scripture can be wrenched out of context. Just a glance at David's life shows he was not suggesting he would never face need or deprivation. We've already seen he faced terrible betrayal and even assassination attempts within his own family, and spent time as a fugitive from the wrath of Saul. The apostle Paul also knew both what it was to be in need, and to have plenty. Christians suffer when famine strikes – we know this from contemporary examples, as well as biblical occasions of scarcity. Jesus shows us that those whom God loves still suffer.

The psalmist was affirming he was content with being with God, and with God's flock. That statement, we know, does create mystery and even frustration, because God's people obviously still suffer. But in a world where suffering and pain are such a reality, I am glad we are not abandoned.

Prayer: I am Yours, and You are mine, and in that reality, I rest, Father. Amen.

Read:
Psalm 23:1
2 Corinthians 11:23–29

FOCUS

'I lack nothing.'
(Psa. 23:1)

Christians suffer

Lessons from lambs

Sheep, being naturally timid and fearful, don't find it easy to lie down and rest. They are easily spooked – the presence of a passing rabbit can startle them. One sheep bolts, and then the flock follow suit, frightened without even knowing the source of concern. They are just afraid because fear is in the air. Other issues hijack their ability to rest, like friction in the flock, or the relentless irritation that parasites and pests bring. Hunger will prevent rest as well. The answer to all of these challenges is the faithful presence of the shepherd. When the shepherd is near, the sheep feel secure.

Study God's interactions with His people, and it's striking to see how many questions God answers with the promise, 'I will be with you.' In Matthew's gospel, as Jesus gives His disciples the Great Commission, He assures them He will be with them, always. Christianity is not about following rules laid out by a distant God, but doing life in the knowledge He is near now, with us, empowering us. In Christ, we will never be alone again. Ever.

To ponder: Is it possible to believe that God is present and with us, but live in way that we would live if there was no God?

'I will be with you.'

Weekend

Perfectly Perplexing

Throughout the last 2000 years, Christians all over the world have sought to adapt Jesus to their own ends; today's Church is no different. All these different versions will hold elements of the true Jesus, even if only faintly, but what does the Bible show us of what He was really like? Jeff Lucas takes us through some of the surprising things Jesus said and did, and explodes some popular misconceptions about Him along the way.

Please note that the Nov/Dec 2021 issue will be the final issue of Life Every Day.

Also available as eBook/eSubscription

Obtain your copy from waverleyabbeyresources.org or a Christian bookshop

Thirst and the shepherd

Read:
Psalm 23:1–2
Psalm 42:1–11

....

FOCUS

'He leads me beside quiet waters.'
(Psa. 23:2)

Sheep, like all living creatures, desperately need water to sustain them. And so, in Bible times, if they wandered off, they would often drink from muddy pools, maybe containing bacteria that could cause disease. But David describes a shepherd who will lead his flocks to still, clean water that will refresh them and not harm them.

In our fallenness, we are often tempted by things that could harm us, ruin us, or enslave us to addiction. The power of seduction is strong. We lie to ourselves, insisting what we want won't do us any harm and, after all, everyone else is sipping at the same pool, aren't they? We'd do well to know everything that is good comes from God – in a sense, He has the franchise on the good stuff. Far from being a cosmic killjoy whose ambition is to ruin our fun and bring religious restrictions to our lives, He has everything that is good, healthy and wholesome. And if we have decided to follow Christ, we are wonderfully ruined, because now, nothing outside of His gifts will truly satisfy. Once we've seen a vision of the kingdom, we can't unsee it. The second-best will not be good enough for us.

Perhaps you feel a longing, and end up trying to satisfy it with polluted water, which could ultimately poison you. Now is the time to wake up, to see through the lie that temptation spins, and know what He offers is fresh, pure, revitalising and life-giving. Let's enjoy what He has for us: it's fresh, pure, and good.

He has everything that is good, healthy and wholesome

Prayer: When bitter water beckons, help me to say close to You, shepherd of my soul. Amen.

The restorer of our souls

When we hear David describing God as the one who restores his soul, we can be tempted to think of restoration in general terms and forget that David, once a shepherd himself, was using language specific to his former vocation. Sheep are very good at getting stuck, having rolled over onto their backs. They stumble, fall, and are unable to get up unaided. Sometimes they find themselves in this position because they are too fat, or even laden down with too much wool. Whatever the reason, 'cast' sheep need the help of a shepherd to get up again, and if he doesn't show up, they can die in just few hours. Frantically and uselessly flailing around in panic, the sheep experience a loss of blood supply to the legs, and gases build up in the rumen. This condition can cause their death, and they are also easy prey for predators. Even the healthiest of sheep can end up this way. The shepherd arrives, and very gently rolls the sheep over – not too quickly – to relieve the gases and help the sheep to begin stumbling its way back into life and mobility.

Some Christian don't give themselves permission to be 'cast down', and feel guilty when they get low or stuck – they feel bad because they feel bad. But if healthy sheep stumble, so do Christians whom we view as strong and confident. The picture of God the shepherd found here shows us He knows we will experience 'cast down' times, and He will respond, not with indifference or impatience, but tenderness and understanding.

Read:
Psalm 23:1–3
Matthew 11:28

FOCUS
'He restores my soul.'
(Psa. 23:3 ESV)

He knows we will experience 'cast down' times

Prayer: I put my hope in God, for I will yet praise Him, my Saviour and my God. Amen.

Our shepherd guide

....

FOCUS

'He guides me along the right paths for his name's sake.'
(Psa. 23:3)

Yesterday we saw that sheep are very prone to be cast down and, when that happens, they're stuck. One of the great challenges of faith is the danger of quietly becoming stuck where we are. Sheep can overgraze the same pasture, and the land can be 'sheeped to death'. They are creatures of habit, when left to their own resources, and not led well by a shepherd. Sheep will destroy vegetation by pawing out the roots. And in barren pastures in biblical lands, parasites multiplied, quickly infecting the entire flock That's why a shepherd's major responsibility was to keep them on the move.

We Christians are called to be pilgrims and pioneers not settlers. We are not called to ask Jesus to come to where we are, but instead, He gives the winsome (and sometimes terrifying) challenge, 'Follow me, and I will make you fishers of men.' The invitation is to go with Him as He goes. It's ironic that some of us find change so difficult, especially changes in our churches.

The shepherd carefully plans the routes for his sheep to follow – and that's true of our shepherding God. He has written purpose over each of our lives, and calls us to get in step with Him. When sheep are healthy, the reputation of the shepherd is good. And as we determine to be a travelling people, navigating change personally and corporately, we point others to the God who wants them to travel with Him too. Let's follow – even when the pathway is through the valley of the shadow of death.

Christians are called to be pilgrims

Prayer: I will not fear the valley, because You have defeated even death, Lord. I will follow You. Amen.

Rod and staff

Read:
Psalm 23:1–4
Matthew 11:29–30

FOCUS

'Your rod and your staff, they comfort me,' (Psa. 23:4)

I remember the time when I was presented with a bishop's staff. It had previously belonged to Bishop Trevor Huddleston, who did much to confront the scourge of apartheid in South Africa, and the person who gave it to me said that I should carry it as a sign of dependency on God. And so I did, until the day when an airline managed to lose it. The staff is a sign of the shepherd's calling, but it was also a weapon. Shepherds in Bible times practised for hours, learning how to throw their staffs with deadly accuracy at predators. They also used the rod to discipline and direct wayward sheep. A good shepherd wouldn't use it to beat the sheep, but rather gently pressed the animal's side with it to nudge it back on track.

I'm glad that God is gentle, and Jesus describes Himself as gentle of heart. I carried that staff because I needed a reminder to stay close to Him. How easy it is to meander off into my own good ideas and intentions. But through the pricking of conscience, the kind but firm rebuke from a friend, the challenge of a scripture – God's gentle care has generally kept me on track, although I certainly share in that sheep-like attribute of wanting to wander off!

Perhaps God is nudging you, whispering to you right now, lovingly trying to corral you away from a disastrous choice. In my experience, usually He chooses whispers over shouts. Let's respond quickly, because those nudges are for our welfare.

Prayer: I am prone to wander. Nudge me, speak to me, keep me on the right path, Holy Spirit. Amen.

God is gentle

A table and some oil

Read:
Psalm 23:1–5
John 10:1–10

FOCUS

*'You prepare a table
before me in the
presence of my
enemies. You anoint
my head with oil.'*
(Psa. 23:5)

It seems like a radical departure from the sheep/
shepherding imagery, doesn't it, as we read about God
preparing a table for us. Sheep don't gather around
tables! It's believed David was referring to a high, flat
plateau of land, perhaps like Table Mountain in South
Africa. The thought here is of a shepherd who goes
ahead, planning, preparing, choosing pasture, and then
carefully clearing it of poisonous weeds which could
harm the flock. It's good to be reminded that, incredibly,
God has plans for each one of us. I've come to believe
the will of God is not a tightrope to balance on, but a field
to play in. His purposes for us are broad, but specific.

And then the shepherd uses oil on the heads of the
sheep. Not only was this to create a barrier between
flies and parasites that could drive sheep to distraction,
bringing disease and death, but the sheep's heads
were greased because they tended to get into head-
butting conflicts. A greased head created less impact,
and when the sheep got into a fight, they glanced off
each other and less damage was done.

Oil is a very common metaphor for the work of the
Holy Spirit. When I spend time with God, asking Him to
strengthen and fill me, I have a greater ability to deal
with the irritations of life, and with irritating believers
(and I can be one of those irritating believers too!)
Spending time alone with God is a good devotional
habit, and equips us to live in the challenges of life,
filled with His Spirit.

God has
plans for
each one
of us

**Prayer: Spirit of God, fill me anew, afresh today. Anoint
my head, my heart, my hands, with the oil of Your Spirit.
Amen.**

What follows us and our future

s we come to the end of our study, we see what happens
hen we allow God to be our shepherd. We create legacy.
egacy is not just what is left when we die. We create
gacy each day in the effect we have on others. Let's
ccept the challenge – do we create peace, or discord?
re others built up because we are in their lives, or do
e sow seeds of confusion or destruction? Being around
od's goodness should create goodness in us.

nd then we hear truth of the eternal shepherd, and
he wondrous hope we have in Him – we too will dwell
n the house of the Lord forever, because of His love,
are and grace. As we ponder the God revealed in the
ook of Psalms, we're reminded that His care will be
nending. May that sure and certain hope inspire
is to live beautifully, as we walk every day in the
resence of the good shepherd who has laid down His
ife for us. And, as always, thank you for joining me in
,ife Every Day.

o ponder: What legacy are you currently leaving?

His care will be unending

New releases from Waverley Abbey Resources

The Bird Who Sang Again

Your life sings to those around you. Judy Moore will inspire you to sing out the messages you were designed to carry, and tell the story you have been uniquely crafted to tell.

Strengthen Your Core

Have you felt a little sluggish in your spiritual practices? Are you yearning for spiritual growth, but you're not too sure how to get there? This book will kickstart your spiritual training regime. In eight workouts for your soul, you'll be roused into action and spurred into your spiritual growth spurt.

The God Files Bible

This colourfully presented Bible – in which each book is styled as a 'file' – will invite children into the story of Scripture by encouraging them to play their part as agents with a mission, inspired by the adventures and impact of the special agents they read about, such as Joseph, David, Esther and Mary.

To find out more about all our new releases, visit

waverleyabbeyresources.org/category/new-releases/

Order form

5 Easy Ways To Order

1. Visit our online store at **waverleyabbeyresources.org/store**
2. Send this form together with your payment to: **Waverley Abbey Resources, Waverley Abbey House, Waverley Lane, Farnham, Surrey GU9 8EP**
3. Phone in your credit card order: **01252 784700** (Mon–Fri, 9.30am – 4.30pm)
4. Visit a Christian bookshop
5. For Australia and New Zealand visit KI Entertainment **kigifts.com.au**

For a list of our National Distributors, who supply countries outside the UK, visit waverleyabbeyresources.org/distributors

Your Details (required for orders and donations)

Full Name: CWR ID No. (if known):

Home Address:

                                                Postcode:

Telephone No. (for queries):   Email:

Publications

TITLE	QTY	PRICE	TOTAL
		Total Publications	

UK P&P: up to £24.99 = **£2.99**; £25.00 and over = **FREE**	
Elsewhere P&P: up to £10 = **£4.95**; £10.01 – £50 = **£6.95**; £50.01 – £99.99 = **£10**; £100 and over = **£30**	
Total Publications and P&P (please allow 14 days for delivery) **A**	

Waverley Abbey Resources Bible Reading notes are also available as single issue **ebooks**.
Visit **waverleyabbeyresources.org** for further information.

Continued overleaf >>

How would you like to hear from us? We would love to keep you up to date on all aspects of the CWR ministry, including; new publications, events & courses as well as how you can support us.

If you **DO** want to hear from us on email, please tick here [ ]

If you **DO NOT** want us to contact you by post, please tick here [ ]

You can update your preferences at any time by contacting our customer services team on 01252 784 700. You can view our privacy policy online at waverleyabbeyresources.org

<< See previous page for start of order form

Payment Details

☐ I enclose a cheque/PO made payable to CWR for the amount of: **£** _____

☐ Please charge my credit/debit card.

Cardholder's Name (in BLOCK CAPITALS) _____

Card No. ☐☐☐☐ ☐☐☐☐ ☐☐☐☐ ☐☐☐☐ ☐☐☐☐

Expires End ☐☐ ☐☐   Security Code ☐☐

Gift to CWR   ☐ Please send me an acknowledgement of my gift   **C** [_____]

Gift Aid (your home address required, see overleaf)

giftaid it I am a UK taxpayer and want CWR to reclaim the tax on all my donations for the four years prior to this ye and on all donations I make from the date of this Gift Aid declaration until further notice.*

Taxpayer's Full Name (in BLOCK CAPITALS) _____

Signature _____   **Date** _____

*I am a UK taxpayer and understand that if I pay less Income Tax and/or Capital Gains Tax than the amount of Gift Aid claimed on all my donations in that year it is my responsibility to pay any difference.

GRAND TOTAL (Total of A, B & C) [_____]

CWR Instruction to your Bank or Building Society to pay by Direct Debit

Please fill in the form and send to: CWR, Waverley Abbey House, Waverley Lane, Farnham, Surrey GU9 8EP

DIREC Deb

Name and full postal address of your Bank or Building Society

To: The Manager   Bank/Building Society

Address _____

_____

_____

          Postcode

Name(s) of Account Holder(s)

[_____]

Branch Sort Code

[☐☐ ☐☐ ☐☐]

Bank/Building Society Account Number

[☐☐☐☐☐☐☐☐]

Originator's Identification Number

| 4 | 2 | 0 | 4 | 8 | 7 |

Reference

[_____]

Instruction to your Bank or Building Society

Please pay CWR Direct Debits from the account detailed in this Inst subject to the safeguards assured by the Direct Debit Guarantee. I understand that this Instruction may remain with CWR and, if so, d will be passed electronically to my Bank/Building Society.

Signature(s)

_____

_____

Date _____

Banks and Building Societies may not accept Direct Debit Instructions for some types of account